Mind Over Money
Psychological Strategies for Wealth Creation

Table of Contents

1. Introduction 1

2. The Psychology of Wealth: An Introduction 2

    2.1. The Power of Perception 2

    2.2. Money and Happiness: A Complex Correlation 2

    2.3. Financial Behavior and Cognitive Bias 3

    2.4. Developing a Wealth Mentality 3

    2.5. Balancing Risk and Reward 4

    2.6. Money Scripts 5

3. Understanding Money Mindsets: Abundance vs. Scarcity 6

    3.1. The Scarcity Mindset 6

    3.2. From Scarcity to Abundance 6

    3.3. The Abundance Mindset 7

    3.4. Abundance in Practice 7

    3.5. Money Mindset and Wealth Creation 8

4. Transforming Your Financial Blueprint: Steps Towards Change . 9

    4.1. Your Current Financial Blueprint 9

    4.2. The Role of Past Experiences 9

    4.3. Identifying Limiting Beliefs 10

    4.4. The Power of Affirmations 10

    4.5. Set Financial Goals 11

    4.6. Create a Wealth Plan 11

    4.7. Implement and Adjust 11

5. Harnessing the Power of Positive Thinking in Finance 13

    5.1. Understanding Positive Psychology and Its Application in Finance 13

    5.2. Emotional Intelligence and Financial Decision Making . 14

    5.3. The Cycle of Positive Financial Behaviors 14

    5.4. The Power of Visualization in Achieving Financial Goals . 15

5.5. Practicing Gratitude and Building Abundance 15

5.6. The Role of Affirmations in Boosting Financial Confidence . . 15

5.7. Shattering Limiting Beliefs About Money 16

5.8. Developing a Financial Growth Mindset 16

5.9. Setting Financial Boundaries: A Positive Approach to

Saying No 17

6. Behavioral Finance: Biases and Heuristics 18

6.1. Cognitive Biases in Investment Decisions 18

6.2. Behavioral Heuristics 19

6.3. The Impact of Bias and Heuristics on Financial Markets 20

6.4. Utilizing an Understanding of Biases and Heuristics 20

6.5. Mitigating Biases and Heuristics 21

7. The Influence of Emotions on Financial Decision Making 22

7.1. The Role of Emotions 22

7.2. Emotion and Financial Behavior: An Overview 22

7.3. The Emotional Roller Coaster: Fear and Greed 23

7.4. 'Regret Aversion': The Past Looms Large 23

7.5. The 'Happiness Dividend' 24

7.6. Tipping the Scales: Balancing Emotion and Logic in

Financial Decisions 24

7.7. Conclusion: Quelling the Emotional Tide 25

8. Psychology-Based Investing: Strategies for Success 26

8.1. The Psychology of Investing 26

8.2. The Role of Cognitive Biases in Investment 26

8.3. The Mind of a Successful Investor 27

8.4. Investing Strategies Rooted in Psychology 28

9. Breaking Free from Financial Fear: Overcoming Anxiety and

Procrastination 30

9.1. Understanding Financial Fear 30

9.2. Managing Financial Anxiety 30

9.3. Overcoming Financial Procrastination 31

9.4. Understanding Procrastination 31

9.5. Combatting Procrastination 32

9.6. Financial Fear to Financial Confidence: Your Journey 32

9.7. Conclusion 33

10. Applying Cognitive Behavioral Techniques in Personal
Finance 34

10.1. How Cognitive Behavioral Techniques Work in Finance . . . 34

10.2. Understanding And Identifying Cognitive Distortions 35

10.3. Improving Financial Behaviors 35

10.4. Creating An Effective Financial Plan 36

10.5. Persisting with Cognitive Behavioral Techniques 36

11. Mental Wealth: Building a Healthy Financial Future 38

11.1. Understanding the Psychology of Money 38

11.2. The Role of Mindset 39

11.3. How Emotions Influence Financial Decisions 39

11.4. Crafting a Positive Relationship With Money 40

11.5. Setting Financial Goals 40

11.6. Money Mindfulness: Present Focus and Future Planning . . . 40

11.7. Putting It All Together: Psychological Strategies for Wealth
Creation 41

Chapter 1. Introduction

Welcome to our latest Special Report, "Mind Over Money: Psychological Strategies for Wealth Creation". Dive into the fascinating crossroads between human psychology and unexpected wealth accumulation right now! This comprehensive compilation unravels the power of your mind in shaping your financial future. Delving into the world of finance might seem complex, but rest assured - this Special Report is structured to be easily digestible, no matter your background. Whether you're a novice or a seasoned investor, our accessible approach guides you through the process, revealing practical strategies you can apply for effective wealth creation. Our aim? To equip you not just with the understanding of techniques, but also the confidence to utilize them to your advantage. Prepare to revolutionize the way you view money, success, and wealth as you embark on this thrilling journey of personal and financial growth.

Chapter 2. The Psychology of Wealth: An Introduction

The human mind is a fascinating entity, capable of the unique ability to shape its surrounding circumstance - the realm of personal finance is no exception. Understanding the intricate dance between psychology and wealth accumulation could serve as a road-map to more prosperous vistas.

2.1. The Power of Perception

The perception of wealth varies dramatically from person to person. This particular bias can impact how we approach our financial journey significantly. For some, wealth is encapsulated within the accumulation of material possessions such as luxury cars and opulent homes. For others, it is the freedom to live life according to their terms - be it travel, time with loved ones, or the freedom to pursue passions. These fundamental differences in perception can greatly influence how we prioritize, spend, and save our money.

Behavioral economic research suggests that our experiences, values, and beliefs play a core role in shaping these perceptions. In effect, one's financial well-being is not just about earning, but also dictated by attitudes and behaviors shaped by our unique experiences. Acknowledging these cognitive biases and triggers is integral to understanding the psychology of wealth.

2.2. Money and Happiness: A Complex Correlation

The age-old adage, "money can't buy happiness," has been extensively studied, and the findings are somewhat conflicting. While money does not directly equate to happiness, financial stability can alleviate stressors and provide a sense of security, both of which contribute to overall well-being.

Research has shown that there is a happiness plateau beyond a certain income level. A seminal study by Daniel Kahneman and Angus Deaton suggested that the average individual's emotional well-being did not increase beyond an annual income of $75,000, hinting at the diminishing returns of wealth accumulation.

Moreover, the joy derived from wealth tends to lean heavily on how it is spent. Expenditure on experiences provides longer lasting happiness than splurging on material possessions, largely because our memories form an integral part of our identities, while material objects depreciate with use and over time.

2.3. Financial Behavior and Cognitive Bias

Our cognitive biases can sometimes steer us astray from making rational financial decisions. For example, the 'recency bias' can cause us to make choices based on recent market trends, forgetting the longer, overall trajectory. The 'confirmation bias' prompts us to favor information that confirms pre-existing beliefs, sidelining potentially important contradictory data.

A foundational understanding of these intrinsic biases allows us to recognize their presence, providing a stepping stone to more rational, calculated decision-making.

2.4. Developing a Wealth Mentality

The idea of a wealth mentality is grounded in shifting from reactive strategies to proactive ones, viewing challenges as opportunities rather than obstacles. In essence, it revolves around fostering a mindset that welcomes abundance, seeks constructive solutions, and sets clear, concise financial goals.

First, nurture a positive attitude towards wealth. View money not as a necessary evil but a tool to open up your options and bring dreams to fruition. Embrace the concept of wealth accumulation as a journey of growth and learning, rather than merely an end goal.

Next, take active control of your financial future. Begin planning and setting feasible financial goals. Regularly assess your financial health, confront and correct any self-defeating beliefs, and implement changes necessary to correct course.

Finally, nurture financial knowledge. Continual learning is a pillar of the wealth psychology. Read, attend seminars, seek mentors - do whatever it takes to gain a good grasp of financial concepts. The more you understand, the better equipped you are to take advantage of opportunities when they arise.

2.5. Balancing Risk and Reward

Mental accounting, a concept coined by Richard Thaler, refers to our tendency to categorize and treat money differently depending on its source, intended use, or amount. This bias can lead to irrational choices; for example, someone might be loath to dip into their savings account to pay off high-interest debt, simply because they categorize one as spending and the other as saving.

Risk tolerance and aversion play crucial roles in our financial decision-making process. The psychology behind this balance varies immensely from one person to another. It's critical to identify your comfort zone regarding risk and reward to make sound investment decisions, simultaneously pushing the limits to optimize gains.

2.6. Money Scripts

Coined by financial psychologist Brad Klontz, a "money script" is a belief about money, often unconscious and learned in childhood, that drives our financial behaviours. There are generally four types: money avoidance, money worship, money status, and money vigilance. Identifying your money script helps uncover misconceptions that might be holding you back from maximizing your financial potential.

In conclusion, the psychology of wealth is a complex and multifaceted subject. It is neither merely about numbers nor solely about mindset, but a crafty blend of the two. The human mind holds immense power to shape our financial trajectories. When armed with awareness of the cognitive corners that might trip us - and the knowledge to sidestep these stumbling blocks - the path to successful wealth accumulation becomes significantly clearer. The voyage will be unique to each of us, but understanding the psychological underpinnings of wealth can help navigate the journey with clarity, purpose, and confidence. Enjoy the journey - for it's as rewarding as the destination.

Chapter 3. Understanding Money Mindsets: Abundance vs. Scarcity

Despite being quite an abstract concept, money is incredibly powerful in shaping our lives and our world. It can determine our status, our lifestyle, and even our happiness. However, one crucial aspect about money often overlooked is the mindset with which we approach it, and how this mindset influences our financial decisions and ultimately, our wealth. In this chapter, we will delve deep into the two core money mindsets: Abundance and Scarcity.

3.1. The Scarcity Mindset

The scarcity mindset is a viewpoint where individuals believe that there are limited resources and opportunities available, leading to a state of fear and constant worry about money. People with this mindset often focus on short-term survival and preservation, rather than long-term economic growth.

Instead of seeking out avenues for wealth creation, they avoid taking risks and spend most of their time worrying about losing the money they have or how they will pay their next bills. They tend to be overly frugal, anticipate worst-case scenarios, and hold back on investments.

3.2. From Scarcity to Abundance

Despite its grim outlook, the scarcity mindset is not a life sentence; it can be shifted to a more productive and positive outlook - the abundance mindset. Recognizing and understanding this mindset is the first step towards shifting one's perspective.

Those with the scarcity mindset can start by challenging their thoughts about money. This involves analysing their assumptions, asking whether they are based in reality or rooted in fear. It is also beneficial to explore their relationship with money: where it started, how it has developed over time, and how it is impacting their present actions. Awareness is crucial in order to begin the process of transforming the mindset.

3.3. The Abundance Mindset

An abundance mindset, on the other hand, is the belief that there is enough to go around for everyone. It focuses on the infinite possibilities and opportunities available, rather than being limited by apparent constraints.

People with the abundance mindset display optimism about the future, exhibit resilience in the face of setbacks, and take calculated risks with hopes of achieving higher rewards. They see potential for growth everywhere and view money as a toolwhich enables them to help themselves and others.

They are more likely to invest, seek out new opportunities, and act proactively to improve their financial situations. Consequently, they are often more successful in making money work for them, rather than working endlessly for money.

3.4. Abundance in Practice

Shaping your mindset to one of abundance does not mean neglecting fiscal responsibility, rather it involves embracing possibilities while maintaining prudent financial habits. Here are a few practical strategies:

1. Be Grateful: Start by appreciating what you already have. This helps shift focus from what is lacking, to the wealth already at

hand.

2. Spend Mindfully: Develop a habit of informed spending. Instead of restricting your spending, focus on getting value for your expenditure.

3. Invest in Yourself: This could involve furthering your education, learning new skills, or investing time into self-care. Remember, you are your greatest asset.

4. Be Generous: Share what you have with others. This reinforces your belief in abundance and creates a positive impact around you.

5. Seek Growth: Continually seek out new opportunities for wealth creation, be it investments, a side hustle or business ventures.

3.5. Money Mindset and Wealth Creation

Ultimately, your mindset plays a critical role in shaping your financial future. It influences your actions, decisions, and habits regarding money. By fostering an abundance mindset, you start to see the wealth of opportunities around you, enabling you to make more informed, deliberate, and beneficial choices in your pursuit of wealth.

Always remember, abundance is about more than just money - it is about personal growth, satisfaction, happiness, and achieving a balanced life filled with wealth in all aspects. So reshape your money mindset and unlock your potential to create a prosperous future.

Chapter 4. Transforming Your Financial Blueprint: Steps Towards Change

Every individual possesses a unique framework for understanding and interacting with finances. This framework, often referred to as a "financial blueprint," is shaped by an assortment of influences, including childhood experiences, societal messages, and personal values. However, much like the blueprint of a house, this mental construct isn't set in stone. Understanding its foundations and actively working towards changing them, if necessary, can dramatically influence your financial path.

4.1. Your Current Financial Blueprint

To start transforming your financial blueprint, you must first identify and understand your current financial beliefs and behaviors. Ask questions to reveal your financial blueprint: When it comes to money, do you act out of fear or greed? Are you prone to risky behavior or extreme caution? Can you invest long-term or do you frequently sell out of anxiety? Document your behaviors, attitudes, and decision-making tendencies. Going through this introspective process can reveal deep-rooted beliefs that may be hindering your wealth accumulation.

4.2. The Role of Past Experiences

The way we think about money and wealth is often deeply rooted in past experiences, particularly those from childhood. Financial habits and attitudes cultivated during these formative years exert far-reaching influences on our adult lives. If you grew up in a family where money was a constant source of tension, you might have unknowingly cultivated a fear-based relationship with money. Conversely, if you were taught that money is a tool for creating comfort and opportunity, you might have a more confident approach towards finances. To revisit these experiences, journal about your earliest memories associated with money. You might uncover patterns that help explain your current financial behavior and attitudes.

4.3. Identifying Limiting Beliefs

Many people unconsciously hold onto limiting beliefs around money that negatively impact their financial wellbeing. Such beliefs could include ideas that rich people are unethical, that you don't deserve abundance, or that money is the root of all evil. However, not all limiting beliefs are negative; some may simply be misguided. Perhaps you've been told that you must work relentlessly to make a good living. Recognizing these beliefs as inhibitive rather than absolute truths is the first step towards change. Consider different instances when these beliefs have manifested in your financial decisions. Upon recognition, you can start to challenge and rewrite these beliefs.

4.4. The Power of Affirmations

Affirmations are positive statements that can help overcome self-sabotaging thoughts. Once you've identified your limiting beliefs, address them using affirmations that speak directly to those hurdles. For example, if you struggle with believing you deserve financial success, an affirmation could be: "I am deserving of abundance and my potential for wealth is limitless." Repeat this affirmation daily or as often as needed. This process allows you to mentally replace destructive thoughts with constructive ones, thereby reprogramming your mind for prosperity.

4.5. Set Financial Goals

Goal setting is a cornerstone of financial success. While transforming your financial blueprint, it's crucial to clearly articulate your financial goals. These goals should be SMART—Specific, Measurable, Achievable, Relevant, and Time-bound. Whether you aim to save a certain sum, reduce debt, or increase your investment portfolio, clear financial goals give you a definitive direction and keep your money habits aligned with your wealth creation path.

4.6. Create a Wealth Plan

After establishing your financial goals, it's time to create a wealth plan—a road map leading you towards your envisioned future. It's essential for this plan to incorporate different elements like debt reduction, investments, savings, and your future income streams. It should also consider inevitable life events like retirement. Tailor your plan to your personal financial situation, risk tolerance, and wealth goals; this may involve seeking professional advice to ensure that all crucial factors are taken into account.

4.7. Implement and Adjust

Taking action is key. Implement your wealth plan and monitor your progress. Adjustments may be necessary as you meet challenges or as your circumstances change. However, resist the urge to abandon your plan during hard times. Having a financial blueprint that aligns with your wealth creation goals will not only provide you with much-needed stability in times of hardship, but it will also reinforce your path towards wealth accumulation.

In summary, transforming your financial blueprint requires self-awareness, commitment to change, setting clear financial goals, creating a realistic wealth plan, and then implementing this plan while staying ready for adjustments. Follow this path, and you're bound to make significant progress in your journey towards financial success. Remember, it's not the amount of money that comes into your life, but how you manage and multiply that money that will truly determine your financial future. It all begins with the transformation of your financial blueprint.

Chapter 5. Harnessing the Power of Positive Thinking in Finance

Positive thinking is not merely an abstract idea that urges us to adopt a merry perspective towards life. In the realm of finance, it's a practical and powerful tool that can unlock a wealth of benefits. Making smart financial decisions isn't just about knowledge and skills, it also involves a positive mindset. In this chapter, we shall delve into the mechanisms through which you can harness the power of positive thinking to achieve your financial goals.

5.1. Understanding Positive Psychology and Its Application in Finance

Positive psychology isn't about wearing rose-colored glasses—it's about strengthening the positive aspects of your character. By focusing on elevating your strengths and cultivating an optimistic outlook, you can achieve greater fulfillment and resilience.

When applied to finance, positive psychology encourages an abundance mindset. Instead of viewing money as a scarce and stress-inducing necessity, you can perceive it as a tool for growth. The beliefs you hold about money often unconsciously steer your financial behaviors. A positive psychological stance situates you to make better financial decisions, enabling you to manage, save, and invest money effectively.

5.2. Emotional Intelligence and Financial Decision Making

Emotional Intelligence (EI) is the ability to understand and manage not only your emotions, but also the emotions of others. When it comes to making financial decisions, EI proves to be a critical skill. Often our money-related decisions are influenced by our emotional state.

A high level of EI enables an individual to separate their emotions from their decisions. This means that instead of making impulsive purchases based on emotional triggers, an emotionally intelligent person will make calculated decisions that are in alignment with their long-term goals.

5.3. The Cycle of Positive Financial Behaviors

Positive thinking in finance is cyclical and serves to reinforce itself. When you adopt a positive mindset, you're more likely to engage in beneficial financial behaviors, such as saving and investing. This, in turn, leads to improved financial outcomes which fuel more positivity, leading to enhanced financial decision-making.

The initial step is adopting a positive outlook towards financial matters. By cultivating beneficial beliefs, financial planning and execution become significantly less daunting, paving the way for opportunistic wealth creation.

5.4. The Power of Visualization in Achieving Financial Goals

The power of visualization is key to harnessing positive thinking in finance. Athletes, artists, and entrepreneurs alike have used visualization to reach dazzling heights. Finance is no different—visualizing your financial goals can subconsciously guide your financial decisions and behaviors towards those visions.

Visualize in detail what achieving your financial goal would look like. What would you do with your accumulated wealth? Study? Travel? Philanthropy? Invest? The more detail you can apply, the more tangible your goal will seem, and the more motivated you will be to attain it.

5.5. Practicing Gratitude and Building Abundance

A key aspect of positive thinking is the practice of gratitude. In finance, this means appreciating what you have now. Cherishing your current financial status—regardless of its size—can help build an abundance mindset.

An abundance mindset encourages you to believe that there are plenty of resources available for everyone. This kind of thinking can alleviate stress related to scarcity and enhance your financial decision-making abilities.

5.6. The Role of Affirmations in Boosting Financial Confidence

Affirmations are positive assertions that you repeat to yourself in order to foster positive change. They reinforce the belief in your abilities and help to build your confidence, which is crucial in the world of finance.

Regularly affirming your capabilities and envisioning your financial goals can result in a major boost to your financial confidence. As your financial confidence grows, it stands to reason that so will your financial capability.

5.7. Shattering Limiting Beliefs About Money

Negative beliefs constrain your financial potential. They can make you doubt your ability to gain wealth, causing you to miss financial opportunities. Shattering these beliefs is essential in unlocking your financial potential.

Start by identifying any negative beliefs about money you might hold. Are you inclined to think that money is the root of all evil? That the wealthy are greedy? That you don't deserve wealth? These beliefs indirectly shape your financial decisions and can obstruct your path to wealth.

Once identified, strive to replace these limiting beliefs with positive ones. This could be as simple as telling yourself that money is a tool for good, the wealthy can be generous, and you deserve prosperity, too.

5.8. Developing a Financial Growth Mindset

A financial growth mindset is characterized by the belief that financial skills and intelligence can be developed. It's associated with a holistic view of money, perceiving setbacks as opportunities for learning, and always striving for improvement.

Developing a financial growth mindset involves regular self-reflection and education. Whether it's learning about investments, budgeting, taxes, or retirement planning, continuous learning equips you to handle a range of financial situations confidently.

5.9. Setting Financial Boundaries: A Positive Approach to Saying No

Setting financial boundaries involves deciding on what you will and won't spend your money on, and sticking to these principles—even if it means saying no to yourself or others. Not only does this promote financial health, it also raises your self-esteem since you're demonstrating respect for your financial future.

In conclusion, it's essential to recognize that your mindset plays a huge role in determining your financial success. Positivity, gratitude, abundance—these are the characters in your psychological makeup that make you resilient in the face of financial trials. They help you see the opportunities for growth where others only see obstacles. By harnessing the power of positive thinking in finance, you're setting yourself up for a future of prosperity and fulfillment. The road to financial enlightenment isn't marked by numbers alone, it's paved with the bricks of a positive mindset.

Chapter 6. Behavioral Finance: Biases and Heuristics

Behavioral finance is a subfield of finance that borrows concepts from psychology to better understand stock market anomalies and asset pricing models. It studies how cognitive psychological biases influence the financial behavior of investors and the consequent impact on the markets. It seeks to combine the study of finance with cognitive psychology to offer explanations as to why people make irrational financial decisions.

6.1. Cognitive Biases in Investment Decisions

Cognitive bias is the systematic error in judgment that occurs when individuals process the available information. Let's look at a few biases that affect investment decisions.

1. **Overconfidence Bias** - This is when traders believe they are better at predicting the stock market than they actually are. Overconfidence often leads to excessive trading as the investor believes they can outsmart the market.

2. **Hindsight Bias** - This is the tendency for people to believe they knew something was going to happen after it has already happened. In finance, it can result in an inflated belief in one's abilities to predict market outcomes, leading to potentially risky investments.

3. **Confirmation Bias** - This is the tendency to focus on information that confirms pre-existing beliefs while ignoring information that contradicts them. In finance, confirmation bias can lead to

overconfidence in the stocks one currently owns or is considering buying.

4. **Availability Bias** - This is the tendency to favor readily available information over comprehensive data. Investors may base decisions on recent news without seeing the big picture.

6.2. Behavioral Heuristics

Behavioral heuristics are decision-making shortcuts that help individuals make quick decisions without analyzing every detail. While these can be helpful in some instances, they can be detrimental to financial decision-making.

1. **Anchoring** - Investors often become "anchored" to a specific price point. Some may resist selling a stock until it reaches their purchase price, even if all evidence suggest it will continue to fall.

2. **Herd Mentality** - This is when investors follow the trends or behaviors of a larger group, often leading to 'bubbles' and 'crashes.' If everyone is buying a certain stock, others may decide to do the same, causing an inflation in its price.

3. **Loss Aversion** - Investors tend to prefer avoiding losses than acquiring equivalent gains. Consequently, they might make poor investment decisions, such as holding on to losing investments for too long in the hope that they'll bounce back.

4. **Representativeness** - Investors often base the likelihood of future outcomes by relating them to past experiences or stereotypes. For example, they may believe that because a company has performed well in the past, it will continue to do so in the future.

6.3. The Impact of Bias and Heuristics on Financial Markets

Researchers in behavioral finance have found that the irrational behavior caused by these biases and heuristics can have significant effects on financial markets. These include stock market overreactions, excessive trading, and market bubbles. These effects can lead to market inefficiencies, which present opportunities for less biased investors to outperform the market.

This isn't a call to completely avoid heuristics and biases when making investment decisions. Some level of bias is needed and heuristics are useful for efficient decision-making. The key is to be mindful of them and to ensure they are not leading to less than optimal investment decisions.

6.4. Utilizing an Understanding of Biases and Heuristics

By understanding our own cognitive biases and heuristics, we can improve our financial decisions. For instance, knowing that we're prone to confirmation bias can push us to actively seek out information that challenges our initial assumptions. Knowing we're susceptible to anchoring, we could make a conscious effort to reevaluate our hold prices.

One strategy to counter our biases is 'nudging.' Nudges are subtle changes in the way options are presented to us, which can help us make better decisions. For instance, individuals tend to save more for retirement when they're automatically enrolled in retirement savings plans. This auto-enrollment is a type of nudge that capitalizes on our inherent inertia and default bias.

Another strategy is to use algorithms or robo-advisors for investment decisions. These algorithms use statistical techniques to determine the best investment strategy and are not influenced by biases or emotions.

For heuristics, it's about knowing when to use them. Quick decision-making shortcuts can be beneficial when investment opportunities are time-sensitive. Yet, without thorough analysis, relying on heuristics can result in poor decisions.

6.5. Mitigating Biases and Heuristics

While recognizing our biases is the first step, mitigating them requires concrete action steps:

1. **Embrace Diverse Opinions** - This combats confirmation bias. Listen to alternate viewpoints and consider all evidence before making decisions.

2. **Stick to a Well-Defined Investment Strategy** - This can prevent overconfidence bias. Establish and stick to your investment criteria.

3. **Reframe the Decision** - Investors can avoid loss aversion by reframing the decision in a gains context rather than a losses context.

4. **Set and Stick to Stop-Loss Points** - This technique can help overcome anchoring and representativeness.

The bottom line is, developing an understanding of these cognitive biases and heuristics could be the key distinguishing factor between making good or poor investment decisions. It is crucial for us to introspect, recognize our weaknesses, and take steps to ensure we don't fall prey to these financial traps.

Chapter 7. The Influence of Emotions on Financial Decision Making

"Choosing to make financial choices solely based on logic and rationale is sage advice drilled into society by financial gurus across the globe. However, the reality remains that beneath the surface of every decision, especially financial ones, emotions play a significant role.

7.1. The Role of Emotions

The landscape of conventional finance is founded on the idea that individuals are rational actors. However, emerging fields such as behavioral economics and behavioral finance challenge this premise by taking into account the indelible influence that emotions have on decision-making. Emotions like fear, greed, regret, and even happiness can and do impact our decisions regarding investment, savings, and other financial activities.

Let's traverse the journey of understanding 'why' and 'how' emotions influence financial decisions.

7.2. Emotion and Financial Behavior: An Overview

Human emotions significantly influence financial behaviors, whether we are conscious of them or not. If you've ever felt a pang of regret after selling a stock that later skyrocketed or a rush of excitement from a successful investment, you've felt the undercurrent of emotions impacting your financial decisions.

Investing can bring out a multitude of emotions, both positive and negative. This psychological involvement has given birth to a whole new field of research known as behavioral finance, which delves into the intersection of psychology and financial behaviors, acknowledging that humans are not always rational actors.

7.3. The Emotional Roller Coaster: Fear and Greed

Fear and greed are the two most powerful emotions that drive investor decisions. The emotions swing like a pendulum, creating market volatility and irregularities.

When the market is doing well, investors may get carried away by greed, ignoring risks and overvaluing assets, leading to a market bubble. Conversely, excessive fear can precipitate a market crash as investors hastily withdraw their investments, undervaluing assets which then sell at a discount.

A practical and recent example is the 2008 global financial crisis: failure to recognize and manage greed led to excessively risky decisions, resulting in a significant market downturn when fear eventually set in.

7.4. 'Regret Aversion': The Past Looms Large

Regret aversion is a theory posited by behavioral economists to explain situations in which people make decisions heavily influenced by an earnest desire to minimize feelings of regret if a negative outcome were to occur.

This phenomenon is pervasive in financial decision-making and can manifest in a variety of ways. For example, some investors may hesitate to sell an underperforming asset in fear of feeling regret if its value were to bounce back. Others, after experiencing a loss, may ascribe to riskier investment strategies hoping to quickly recoup their losses, so they don't regret their initial loss.

7.5. The 'Happiness Dividend'

An often-overlooked aspect of financial decision-making is the pursuit of happiness. Research has shown that spending money on experiences that align with one's personalities, such as travel or acquiring a new skill, can create longer-lasting happiness than purchasing material goods. Therefore, individuals must consider the potential 'happiness dividend' when making financial decisions.

7.6. Tipping the Scales: Balancing Emotion and Logic in Financial Decisions

In the ideal world, we would meticulously calculate potential risks and returns before making any financial decision. Unfortunately, our often ephemeral emotional states and biases can sway our decision-making process. This isn't necessarily a bad thing. Emotions can lead to positive outcomes, like the sense of financial security and satisfaction felt in saving for retirement, or the joy of investing in a startup that aligns with your values.

The key lies in acknowledging the emotional element of financial decision-making and finding ways to balance it with appropriate financial knowledge. To achieve this balance, be aware of your emotions, understand your cognitive biases, develop a solid financial plan, regularly review and adjust your investments, and consider taking professional financial advice.

7.7. Conclusion: Quelling the Emotional Tide

Analyzing the relationship between our emotions and financial decision-making can give us keen insights into why we make the choices we do and how we can make better ones. By understanding how emotions influence our decisions, we can put checks in place to prevent emotional decision-making in finance, making more informed choices that ultimately lead to wealth creation."

Chapter 8. Psychology-Based Investing: Strategies for Success

Understanding the cognitive biases, emotions, and psychological factors that influence investment decisions can significantly affect the success of your investment strategy. Let's engage with this insight in-depth.

8.1. The Psychology of Investing

Investment is as much about emotions and psychology as it is about markets and money. Every buy, sell, or hold decision we make is influenced by our beliefs, experiences, bias, and emotions. The world of psychology provides us with a rich array of tools to comprehend these mechanisms better.

Renowned behavioral economists, Daniel Kahneman and Amos Tversky's Prospect Theory, brought the idea into the limelight. The theory essentially states that individuals make decisions based on potential gains or losses rather than final outcomes and often these decisions are irrational.

8.2. The Role of Cognitive Biases in Investment

A cognitive bias is a systematic deviation from rational judgment, causing individuals to behave irrationally. In the investment arena, cognitive biases can be detrimental, impacting decision-making capacity and leading to potential financial losses.

Here are some common cognitive biases seen in investors:

-. Overconfidence bias: This cognitive bias causes individuals to overestimate their abilities and knowledge. They often exhibit a higher risk-tolerance level, engaging in frequent trading and speculative investments.

-. Confirmation bias: Investors subject to this bias seek out and prioritize information that confirms their existing beliefs, often leading to unbalanced investment decisions.

-. Loss aversion: Generally, investors feel the pain of loss more intensely than the joy of an equivalent gain. This bias causes investors to hold onto their losing investments for too long, hoping for a rebound.

-. Herd bias: It refers to the tendency of investors to follow the crowd, often leading to investment bubbles and market crashes.

-. Recency bias: Investors influenced by this bias base their investment decisions on recent news or trends without considering long-term historical data.

Addressing these biases is paramount for improving investment outcomes.

8.3. The Mind of a Successful Investor

A successful investor isn't just someone with a solid knowledge of financial markets or excellent analytical skills. Emotional control, discipline, and long-term perspective are also vital components.

-. Objectivity: A successful investor remains detached from the short-term market swings and focuses on long-term investment goals.

-. Patience: Great investments take time to mature and generate returns. Patience refers to the ability to tolerate time lapses in the face of uncertain outcomes.

-. Risk Management: Investors need to learn how to manage, tolerate, and think about risk rationally.

-. Emotional Control: The ability to separate emotional responses from the investment decision process is vital.

-. Flexibility: A successful investor adapts to changing market conditions, revising strategies as needed.

8.4. Investing Strategies Rooted in Psychology

Integrating psychological insights into your investing strategy can positively impact your wealth creation journey.

-. Dollar-Cost Averaging (DCA): This strategy involves investing a fixed amount of money at regular intervals irrespective of the asset's price. It takes the emotion out of investing and instills discipline.

-. Value Investing: The mindset behind value investing is to treat stock investment like owning a part of the business. Value investors ignore market hype and focus on long-term growth prospects.

-. Rule-Bound Investing: Creating a rule-based investment strategy (like asset allocation rules, selling rules, etc.) can help investors remain objective and disciplined.

-. Emotional Diversification: Not placing all your emotional eggs in one basket is as important as financial diversification. Don't let a single investment or asset class dominate your mental space.

-. Contrarian Investing: This strategy is about going against the crowd. Contrarians purchase assets disparaged by others when they believe the market has overreacted.

The field of behavioral finance is vast and growing. As we continue to delve into the mind of the investor, it becomes increasingly clear that psychology plays a significant role in our financial decisions. A deep understanding of the confluence of psychology and investing can impart a distinctive capability to generate wealth.

Chapter 9. Breaking Free from Financial Fear: Overcoming Anxiety and Procrastination

Fear is often considered the antithesis to progress. When it comes to finances, fear can keep you locked in detrimental financial habits, causing procrastination and perpetuating a cycle of anxiety. In contrast, freedom from financial fear enables the creation of a strong, sensible, and sustainable financial future.

9.1. Understanding Financial Fear

To overcome fear, it's first crucial to identify and understand its origins. Financial fear often comes from a lack of knowledge, prior negative experiences, or societal pressure. As humans, we fear the unknown. Hence, finances become daunting if we lack proper education on managing them. Second, negative past experiences related to money, like a failed investment or massive debt, can instill fear of similar future circumstances. Lastly, societal pressure to 'keep up with the Joneses' can cause financial anxiety, especially when income does not match expense levels.

Yet, no matter how substantial our financial fears, they mustn't dictate our actions.

9.2. Managing Financial Anxiety

Fears can be tamed, and anxiety can be managed. It takes a mindful approach towards understanding and rewiring thoughts about money. Here is a step-by-step plan to manage financial anxiety:

1. Acknowledge: The first step is acceptance. Acknowledge your fear instead of denying it. Once a fear is recognized, it can be processed and eventually overcome.

2. Educate: The enemy of fear is knowledge. Seek financial education to understand the basics of savings, investments, and financial planning. Knowledge will dispel the fear of the unknown and make you more confident in your financial decisions.

3. Therapy: Use therapeutic techniques such as mindfulness, meditation, and Cognitive-Behavioral Therapy (CBT) to mitigate anxiety. These techniques can help you identify negative thought patterns and replace them with positive ones.

4. Talk: Share your fear. Talking about your anxieties can lessen their burden and provide new insights. It also helps build your support network.

5. Plan: Chart out a flexible financial plan. Having a roadmap reduces anxiety about the future.

6. Seek Professional Guidance: Enlisting the help of financial advisors can give you insights and assurance from an experienced perspective.

9.3. Overcoming Financial Procrastination

Financial procrastination, or the tendency to put off financial decisions, is another byproduct of financial fear. Overcoming it requires changing your emotional and mental associations with money and inculcating new, healthier habits.

9.4. Understanding Procrastination

Procrastination seems to be a modern pandemic. Given its

prevalence, it's crucial to understand the mechanics behind it. Essentially, procrastination is an avoidance strategy. It's the result of the mind preferring to deal with immediate gratification rather than face tasks that may lead to discomfort or anxiety. In terms of finances, this could mean deciding to spend money now because it feels good and repeatedly putting off making that long-term investment plan.

9.5. Combatting Procrastination

1. Breakdown Tasks: Large tasks can seem overwhelming. It's better to break them down into manageable subtasks. This makes the process less intimidating and promotes a sense of accomplishment.

2. Set Goals: Setting clear, achievable goals can be a great motivator. Setting financial goals is no exception. Goals play a critical role in guiding your financial decisions and keeping you on track.

3. Implement Deadlines: Deadlines serve two purposes: they provide a timeframe which encourages action, and they offer a sense of urgency that inhibits delay.

4. Positive Reinforcement: Reward yourself for accomplishing financial tasks. This creates a positive feedback loop, making you more likely to complete future tasks.

5. Utilize Digital Tools: There are numerous finance apps and online budgeting tools to help manage your finances. They can automate tasks like bill payments and savings, thus reducing the room for procrastination.

9.6. Financial Fear to Financial Confidence: Your Journey

Having strategies to combat financial fear and procrastination is one thing. Implementing them is another. The shift from fear to confidence is a journey, not an event. It requires consistent effort, awareness, and resilience. Perhaps initially, you might find only short-lived success or encounter setbacks. However, remember, each step you take towards financial strength is a step in the right direction.

9.7. Conclusion

Breaking free from financial fear and overcoming procrastination is crucial for effective wealth creation. By understanding and managing your financial fears and taking active steps to combat procrastination, you can build a fearless and proactive approach towards your finances. This shift from anxiety and delay to confidence and action could be the key to unlocking your financial potential.

Remember, your financial destiny is in your hands. You have the power to change the narrative. Let's step out of our financial fears and stride towards our financial dreams.

Chapter 10. Applying Cognitive Behavioral Techniques in Personal Finance

Understanding cognitive behavioral techniques (CBT) can be transformative in our ability to manage our finances effectively. CBT, originally developed to treat mental health disorders, has seen wider application in other areas of life, including personal finance. It can enable us to recognize – and subsequently alter – cognitive distortions and behaviors that may negatively impact our financial habits and decisions.

10.1. How Cognitive Behavioral Techniques Work in Finance

Cognitive Behavioral Techniques emphasize the role of thinking patterns and beliefs in how we feel and what we do. It suggests that our thoughts about a situation influence our perception, emotional response, and behaviour, which in turn affect the outcome. The objective of using these techniques in a financial context is to make changes that elevate our ability to manage money, multiply wealth, and reach financial goals.

Often, our financial decisions are influenced - or swayed - by our cognitive biases, which are systematic errors in our thinking. These biases make us unknowingly divert from rational judgement. Examples are impulsive spending due to instant gratification bias, obsessing over losses from sunk cost fallacy, or getting overexcited about an investment due to confirmation bias. Cognitive Behavioral Techniques help to correct such biases, leading to intelligent financial decisions.

10.2. Understanding And Identifying Cognitive Distortions

The first step towards implementing CBT in personal finance is identifying cognitive distortions, which can be defined as biased perspectives we have about ourselves and the world around us. They are irrational thoughts and beliefs that we unknowingly reinforce over time.

There are several types of cognitive distortions, including Catastrophizing (assuming the worst-case scenario will always occur), All-or-Nothing Thinking (viewing events in only absolutes, like total success or failure), and Overgeneralizing (basing a decision on a single event and applying it broadly). Such distortions can undermine our subjective judgement about financial decisions.

To rectify these, we can follow these steps: Firstly, become aware of your distortions. Reflect on your financial decisions and pinpoint where your judgement was swayed by biases. Secondly, challenge these distortions. Counter the irrational thoughts with rational ones. Lastly, replace the negatives with positives. Use rational and positive views to reframe the cognitive distortions.

10.3. Improving Financial Behaviors

Once we identify and challenge our cognitive distortions, the next step is to replace them with positive financial behaviors. It's not just about "stopping" a bad habit; it's about substituting it with a beneficial one.

For instance, if you tend to spend money impulsively, don't simply try to stop this behavior. Instead, work on implementing a new behavior – such as saving a part of your disposable income. Using the

S.M.A.R.T (Specific, Measurable, Achievable, Relevant, Time-Bound) framework can be an effective way to ensure your behavioral change is tracked and measured over time.

10.4. Creating An Effective Financial Plan

With cognitive distortions identified and positive financial behaviors underway, another critical aspect to wealth creation is having a powerful financial plan. A plan keeps us focused and ensures our financial decisions align with our long-term wealth creation goals.

Your plan should make clear:

- The reason behind each financial move

- The specific goal of your investments

- Your strategies to curb impulsive spending

- Emergency funds for unforeseen events

Once your plan is ready, implement it and revise it periodically, making changes as necessary to keep it relevant with your evolving financial situation and goals.

10.5. Persisting with Cognitive Behavioral Techniques

As you employ CBT for your personal finances, remember, change is a gradual process. It takes time for new methods to take effect and become habitual. Accordingly, keep these pointers in mind:

- Be patient: Allow time for new behaviors to be deeply ingrained.

- Be consistent: The key to effectively changing your financial behaviors is consistency.

- Reflect and Learn: Take regular stock of your financial progress. What is working? What isn't? Don't be hard on yourself when you experience setbacks. Instead, learn from them to steer your path more effectively moving forward.

In conclusion, Cognitive Behavioral Techniques offer a promising approach to managing your personal finance issues. The awareness and control these techniques provide over psychological biases can bring about significant improvements in financial behaviors and decisions. With patience, consistency, and continuous learning, you will find yourself on the path to sustainable wealth creation.

Chapter 11. Mental Wealth: Building a Healthy Financial Future

Understanding the psychology involved in wealth creation is a fundamental first step toward building a healthy financial future. It is not merely about the money you earn, but also about your beliefs, perceptions, behaviors, and decisions regarding money and wealth. This chapter is designed to provide you with comprehensive knowledge and effective psychological strategies that motivate wealth creation.

11.1. Understanding the Psychology of Money

Our relationship with money and wealth starts at a very young age; we are influenced by various factors such as family background, environment, and cultural upbringing. Negative experiences and inherited narratives can cultivate a sense of scarcity, hindering our ability to create wealth. Understanding these factors is critical to resetting our money mindset.

Three fundamental psychological constructs shape our relationship with money: beliefs, attitudes, and behaviors. Beliefs are the core thoughts we hold about money, while attitudes are our feelings towards money, which are often rooted in our beliefs. Finally, behaviors are the actions we take concerning money, reflecting our beliefs and attitudes.

11.2. The Role of Mindset

Developing the right mindset is instrumental in building wealth. The 'growth mindset,' a concept coined by psychologist Carol Dweck, is an outlook where challenges are viewed as opportunities for improvement, hardships as ways to strengthen resolve, and effort as the path to mastery. A fixed mindset, on the other hand, is an outlook where challenges are construed as threats, hardships as confirmation of inadequacy, and effort as futile if genius is not inherently present.

To cultivate a growth mindset related to wealth: - acknowledge and understand your money beliefs and attitudes - strive to learn more about finance and wealth - perceive challenges as opportunities for growth - make the effort to plan and manage finances

11.3. How Emotions Influence Financial Decisions

Emotions play a critical role in financial decision-making. They can sway our choices and actions, often leading to results that might not align with our long-term financial goals. Awareness of the emotions that drive financial decisions can help us manage them better and make more informed choices.

The common emotions that impact financial decision-making are fear, greed, regret, and overconfidence. Fear might prevent us from taking calculated risks; greed might lure us into unsustainable investments; regret often makes us hold on to losing investments, hoping they'll rebound; overconfidence can lead to hasty, uninformed decisions.

11.4. Crafting a Positive Relationship With Money

Many of us harbor negative associations with money due to past experiences or incorrect beliefs. Shifting those beliefs and building a positive relationship with money is crucial for wealth creation.

To create a positive relationship with money: - appreciate money for what it allows you to do - let go of guilt or fear associated with having money - treat money as a tool, not an end goal - invest in understanding money and finance

11.5. Setting Financial Goals

Setting financial goals can guide you towards building wealth. The goal-setting process should be SMART - Specific, Measurable, Attainable, Relevant, and Time-bound.

Examples of good financial goals are: - building an emergency fund within one year - saving for a home down payment in three years - retiring with $1 million in assets in ten years

11.6. Money Mindfulness: Present Focus and Future Planning

Practicing mindfulness with money means staying present in your financial decisions while keeping your long-term financial goals into consideration. It involves being aware of every financial decision and understanding its impact on future financial health.

11.7. Putting It All Together: Psychological Strategies for Wealth Creation

With an understanding of money psychology, the right mindset, control over emotions, a positive relationship with money, SMART financial goals, and money mindfulness, you are equipped to make better financial decisions and create wealth.

Remember, building wealth is a journey, and these strategies form the roadmap. Understanding your unique financial situation, continuously learning, adapting, and applying these principles will help you create a healthy financial future.

www.ingramcontent.com/pod-product-compliance
Lightning Source LLC
Chambersburg PA
CBHW062308290526
45794CB00006B/2727